Clickers in the Classroom

How to Enhance Science Teaching Using Classroom Response Systems

Douglas Duncan
University of Colorado

Foreword
by Eric Mazur
Harvard University

San Francisco   Boston   New York
Cape Town   Hong Kong   London   Madrid   Mexico City
Montreal   Munich   Paris   Singapore   Sydney   Tokyo   Toronto

Senior Executive Editor: Adam Black
Assistant Editor: Stacie Kent
Senior Marketing Manager: Christy Lawrence
Managing Editor, Production: Erin Gregg
Production Management, Text Design, and Composition:
   Elm Street Publishing Services, Inc.
Manufacturing Manager: Pam Augspurger
Cover Design: Armen Kojoyian
Text and Cover Printer: Courier, Stoughton

Cover Credits: Classroom: Patrick Ward/Corbis, Instructor: Barry
                Rosenthal /Getty

ISBN : 0-8053-8728-5

2 3 4 5 6 7 8 9 10—CRS—08 07 06 05
www.aw-bc.com

Contents

Foreword

Have you ever found yourself standing in front of your class in the middle of a lecture and wondering what in the world is going on in the minds of your students? You look around the classroom. Some students are busy scribbling in their notebooks. A few are dozing off. Many are staring blankly at the screen or blackboard. Or are they just daydreaming? You pause and ask, "Does anyone have any questions?" Silence. Those who were scribbling continue to scribble. The ones who were staring at the screen look down when they notice you looking in their direction. The ones who were dozing off now seem to be fast asleep. "Any questions?" you repeat. The lack of response is agonizing. What is going on in their minds? Did they all understand what you just told them, or are they so totally lost that they don't even know what to ask? If you are like me, chances are you will assume they are all right with the material and move on with the lecture. Most lectures are a one-way transfer of information from the lecturer to the students, and I discovered the hard way that this one-way transfer is very ineffective at helping students master information.

It doesn't have to be that way even if you have hundreds of students in your class. When I first developed the Peer Instruction method, the idea was to find a way to engage the students during class and provide myself (and them) with feedback about their understanding. Initially we used a show of hands, then flashcards. In 1993 we began experimenting with a wired network of handheld calculators to poll the students. Now, a number of commercial systems are available, and tens of thousands of students are being polled each day using wireless devices. The reasons for the explosive growth are simple: First, interactive teaching has been demonstrated to lead to considerably larger learning gains; second, after an instructor has been exposed to the feedback this method of teaching affords, it is impossible to go back to the passive lecture format and remain ignorant about what goes on in the minds of students.

If you have never taught interactively, this book will introduce you to interactive teaching and to the technology that is currently available to support this method. It will also provide you with a treasure chest of tips and pointers. Even if you are already using "clickers," as they are often referred to, you will find the material in this book to be invaluable and will discover new ways of improving your teaching technique. In either case, this book is bound to change your classes, and I am sure you will enjoy reading it as much as I did.

Eric Mazur
Harvard University

About the Author

Douglas Duncan is a faculty member in the Department of Astrophysical and Planetary Sciences of the University of Colorado, where he directs the Sommers Bausch Observatory and Fiske Planetarium. Doug began his career at the Carnegie Observatories and subsequently joined the staff of the Hubble Space Telescope. He then worked at the University of Chicago and the Adler Planetarium, beginning a trend of modernization and closer connection between research and teaching in planetariums, which has spread nationwide. He has served as National Education Coordinator for the American Astronomical Society, and in that capacity led efforts for better teaching and public communication throughout the United States. He has also served as a science commentator on National Public Radio. Doug's current focus is science education and research into "fossil stars"—stars which date back almost to the Big Bang.

Acknowledgments

I am pleased to dedicate this book to Mike Dubson, "father" of clickers at the University of Colorado and an unfailingly helpful and optimistic colleague— as well as the kind of science teacher all students should have. I'd like to give special thanks to Richard Rogers of the Provost's office of the University of Massachusetts, Amherst, for sharing the results obtained with clickers at UMass, and to April Trees and Michelle Jackson for sharing the results of their survey of 1,500 University of Colorado students.

My journey towards better science teaching was started years ago by Amy Southon, a particularly insightful and courageous educator, who challenged me to show whether all those smiling students leaving my lectures were learning what I wanted them to. It took me a decade, Amy, but now I know.

At CU I am privileged to have a remarkable group of colleagues who are truly dedicated and imaginative in their teaching. These include Fran Bagenal, Webster Cash, Erica Ellingson, Jason Glenn, Jim Green, Nick Gnedin, Dick McCray, Bob Pappalardo, Nick Schneider, John Stocke, Ted Snow, and Juri Toomre. Thanks also go to Noah Finkelstein, Steve Pollock, Kathy Perkins, Patricia Rankin, and Carl Weiman.

Eric Mazur at Harvard; Tim Slater and Gina Brissenden of the Conceptual Astronomy and Physics Education Research Team at the University of Arizona; Lorrie Shepard, Dean of Education at the University of Colorado; and Mary Ann Shea, Director of the Faculty Teaching Excellence Program— thank you for your inspiration. Thank you for the valuable feedback and suggestions I received from a number of reviewers including Javed Iqbal (University of British Columbia).

Adam Black, Stacie Kent, and Erin Gregg at Addison-Wesley believed my assertion that there is a lot more to clickers than pushing a button, and then helped me to produce a book I hope has broad appeal. When you are ready to write your own book, see them. They are terrific.

Finally, I am most pleased to thank all my students and teaching assistants in the courses I taught at the University of Chicago and now teach at the University of Colorado. Your thoughts, questions, and enthusiasm have challenged and motivated me.

Douglas Duncan
University of Colorado

Introduction

Introduction—Opportunities

You're a good teacher. You really care about whether your students learn. So as you lecture you watch their faces for clues and ask yourself, "Do they get it? Are they enthusiastic about what I'm saying?" You stop and ask them, "Does anybody have any questions?" Students nervously look at each other. No one raises a hand. Good, you think to yourself, no one had a question—they must be following my presentation and understanding the subject.

If you're an experienced teacher, you know you shouldn't make that assumption. Many students will not call attention to what they don't know, especially in a large class. Research shows that instructors usually overestimate how much students learn. But now, *there's a better way!* Technology has advanced to the point where classroom response systems—or "clickers"—allow a teacher to sample the thinking of all students, at any time, without students having to risk embarrassing themselves in front of their peers.

Here's how the clicker system works. Each student has a transmitter (clicker) that looks very much like a small TV remote control. The clicker has a number of buttons labeled, for instance, a, b, c, d, and e. The classroom has one or more receivers that pick up the signals generated when a student pushes one of the buttons, and a computer equipped with appropriate software to record each student's response. Class results are usually presented without student names attached, typically as a bar chart that can be projected in front of the classroom showing how many students answered a, b, c, d, and e.

Experience shows that the use of clickers *transforms* the classroom, mostly in very positive ways. Student involvement increases. Students are suddenly active participants in class, not merely passive listeners to a lecture. As described in Chapter 6, "Clickers and Cooperative or Peer Instruction," when students are allowed to discuss their answers with their neighbors before responding, the impact is even stronger. Another benefit is that class attendance increases. For instance, the University of Colorado astronomy, planetary science, and physics faculty found that class attendance increased substantially, from 60–70% to 80–90%, after the introduction of clickers. The Illinois Institute of Technology (Burnstein & Lederman, 2001) reported 80–90% attendance in classes where clickers were used. Similar results have been reported from other universities. An important additional advantage to using clickers is that most faculty members enjoy the extra energy, variety, and student involvement clickers bring to a classroom.

Like any technology, though, clickers can be misused. This book will help you enjoy the benefits of clickers while avoiding the pitfalls. The wise use of clickers will help you:

a. Measure what students know before you start to teach them (pre-assessment)
b. Measure student attitudes
c. Find out if the students have done the reading
d. Get students to confront common misconceptions
e. Transform the way you do demonstrations
f. Increase students' retention of what you teach
g. Test students' understanding
h. Make some kinds of grading and assessment easier
i. Facilitate testing of conceptual understanding
j. Facilitate discussion and peer instruction
k. Increase class attendance

The remainder of this book highlights how clickers can help you meet your own goals in teaching while avoiding pitfalls we've seen in clicker systems. See your Addison-Wesley/Benjamin-Cummings sales representative for more information on ready-to-use questions with clickers in your particular course and technology packages they can offer you and your students.

You don't need to be an expert teacher to use clickers. You may be brand new. Or, you may be a busy researcher without a lot of time to devote to teaching, but someone who wants her or his students to really learn science. In either case, this book is for you.

While clickers may be reasonably simple to use, the benefit you and your students derive depends substantially on how you and they use them. If you restrict yourself to factual recall questions and have students answer individually, your students will concentrate on memorizing facts and may consider clicker use a waste of time. If, instead, you follow the recommendations of Chapter 6 and use clickers to facilitate peer discussions and conceptual thinking, your students' learning will be deeper and their enthusiasm will be much greater.

What to Expect

As mentioned before, clickers will transform your classroom. While doing so, they may also contradict the expectations of your students (if they haven't had a "clicker class" before); and a surprised student is not necessarily a happy student. Suddenly, their absences from class are automatically record- ed. Students can't sit in the back of a large lecture hall not paying attention (or sleeping) when every student is questioned and answers are recorded sev- eral times per class. Don't expect students to automatically welcome these changes. It is essential that you discuss with them the benefits clickers bring; otherwise they may concentrate on the disadvantages and be unhappy.

The use of clickers with conceptually based questions or peer discussions, both of which we recommend, strikes at an even more fundamental expecta- tion—what it *means* to learn. Many science classes are still taught in such a way that students can memorize what the teacher says and then later repeat this on an exam and earn an excellent grade. These students often think they've mastered a subject. Scientists know, however, that genuine under- standing means taking a concept and applying it to different situations or dif- ferent kinds of problems, and being able to explain it to someone else. Clickers make it relatively easy to test, immediately, if students can do so. Once again, we recommend that you discuss with your class what you expect them to know before you start testing their knowledge.

An excellent strategy with clickers is to ask thought-provoking questions and evaluate the responses. If the class is split among several different answers, tell students you are going to give them another chance to answer, but first they should turn to their right and left and discuss with their neigh- bors what the correct answer should be. As experienced learners know, explaining something to someone else is a great way to develop your own understanding. But pause to consider what you've done: You've just told students to *talk during class*. You are contradicting years of their schooling, and when you first suggest it, students will often think you don't really mean it. Once they discover you are serious, the classroom will erupt into animated discussion, so much so that you will probably have to raise your voice to get their attention again. As Mazur (1997) observes, these discus- sions usually move the group toward the correct answer rather than an incorrect one, and student understanding and retention increase tremen- dously. However, the active classroom—one that uses clickers, or one that uses clickers plus discussion—requires more effort than sitting and copying notes, which may surprise students. Chapter 9 discusses student opinions.

Since the changes described above are disconcerting to many students, even as they improve students' learning, it is *imperative* that you discuss your expectations of clicker use at the beginning of a term. Tell the students why they will be using them, and how they will benefit. Tell them what you consider cheating when using clickers. Explain the topics discussed in Chapter 2, Why Use a Classroom Response System, and follow the checklist in Chapter 11. You and your students will be much happier.

This book is designed to help you get the most out of clicker use. The University of Colorado began using clickers in 2002 and by the spring of 2004 used 6,000 per semester. At the University of Massachusetts, Amherst, 8,000 were in use in the spring of 2004. Use is spreading quickly, and most faculty members are happy with the results. Survey results from these universities and others are presented later in this book. Chapter 2 presents reasons you should use clickers and how student learning is likely to increase as a result. Chapter 9 presents evidence that students believe clickers improve their learning and that most students enjoy using them—when they are used wisely. Some references are given for further reading and for more detailed data on student performance. The main goal of this book, though, is to be self-contained and immediately practical. Follow the advice here and you can use clickers well. They can be one of the most effective and exciting additions to teaching that you've seen in many years. Good luck!

2

Why Use a Classroom Response System?

Key Points

- Limitations of traditional lectures
- Engaging students in peer discussions
- Learning gains you can expect
- Attitude gains you can expect
- Instructors' opinions about using clickers

Limitations of Traditional Lectures

No matter how good a teacher you are, if you teach solely by lecture, you will lose the attention of many of your students just minutes or tens of minutes after your lecture has begun. An interactive system such as clickers can maintain a much higher level of student involvement.

Teachers strive to be clear and understandable, to motivate and inspire their students. We do so at least in part because we expect that it will help our students learn. Certainly a dull, unclear presentation will discourage students and prevent their learning. But it is also true that *the lecture format itself* imposes limitations on one's ability to teach. Data show very clearly that the success of even an exemplary lecture is limited by the way students learn.

One basic limitation is the attention span of passive learners. Studies indicate that the full attention of students falls off remarkably quickly—in just minutes. IBM performed a study in which the students had strong motivation to learn: All were newly appointed managers, and the classes, taught at IBM headquarters, were an essential part of their jobs. Five classes of 20 students each were studied. Because IBM considered it important that all these students did well, the company carefully studied many aspects of the classes. Observers found that at the beginning of each class, most students exhibited attentive behavior, but that attention diminished rapidly within 20 minutes. Observers watched each student and marked whether he or she was attentive, which formed an index that was equal to 100 when every student was paying attention, 50 when half were, and so on. The average number of students paying attention during a standard lecture was 47. When the lecture was changed to a style in which the teacher actively engaged students with questions, the attention average rose to 68. The observers also noted that in a typical class, 10–20% of the students dominated the discussion. The remaining 80–90% contributed only occasionally. In an effort to improve students' participation, IBM built a prototype interactive classroom in which a student response system allowed every student to respond to teachers' questions. A computer system immediately displayed student responses in graphical form. When the same criteria used to measure students' attentiveness was applied to the classroom with student response units, the attentiveness index was found to be 83. Testing showed that the students in the class with the response system scored significantly higher than the students in the traditional classroom. Students were asked to rate how much they liked the response system, on a scale from 1 to 7, and the average was 6.6. More detail may be found in Horowitz (1988).

IBM conducted the tests described above in 1984–85. Twenty years later, technology has advanced greatly and classroom response systems are available at a fraction of the cost of the IBM prototype. But the way students learn has not changed, and studies in universities have documented that the "fade" in attention during a lecture is a universal phenomenon. Teachers can deal with this by using classroom response systems to "fight the fade" (cf. Pollock, 2004).

For more evidence that traditional lectures fail to produce as much long-lasting learning as we would like, consider the following example from Nobel Laureate Carl Weiman (2004). Weiman is a strong advocate of the use of clickers during lectures and demonstrations. He reports the following example of trying to teach how a violin works—that the body of a violin is essential for amplifying the sound of the strings. Most students have the misconception (or preconception) that the strings make all the sound.

> Explaining about sound and how a violin works. I show class a violin and tell them that the strings cannot move enough air to produce much sound, so actually the sound comes from the wood in the back. Point inside violin to show how there is a sound post so strings can move the

bridge and sound post causes back of violin to move and make sound. 15 minutes later in the lecture I asked students a question—the sound they hear from a violin is produced by a. mostly strings, b. mostly by the wood in the violin back, c. both equally, d. none of the above.

Your multiple-choice question is: What fraction of students do you think got the correct answer?

a. 0%
b. 10%
c. 30%
d. 70%
e. 90%

Test your own expectations and choose a, b, c, d, or e. Remember that the question was asked just 15 minutes later, and in the same lecture that the material was taught.

The result was "b." Only 10% of students gave the correct answer. This is a dramatic example of what is now widely known: An explanation, even a good, clear one (in this case with a demonstration!) often fails to reach students who have misconceptions. Something more active is needed.

Engaging Students in Peer Discussions

Clickers are useful in fighting the "fade" of attention that occurs during lectures. Engaging students can mean more than just holding their attention, however. Clickers are ideally suited to bring about more student involvement through peer instruction or peer discussion. In this approach, teachers use clickers to survey student answers to a thought-provoking conceptual question. If the classroom response system indicates a diversity of opinion, teachers give students several minutes to discuss the question with their neighbors in the lecture hall. It has long been known that teaching someone else helps to understand an idea, and compelling evidence presented in Chapter 6 shows that this relatively easy-to-implement technique can significantly increase student learning. Appendix 2 presents evidence that peer instruction can also greatly raise interest in and enjoyment of science among nonscience majors.

As the photographs show, lecturing has not changed much in two millennia. With the advent of classroom response systems, however, that need not remain the case.

Ancient lecture hall (Photo: © Mimmo Jodice/ CORBIS)

Modern lecture hall (Photo: © Patrick Ward/ CORBIS)

Learning Gains You Can Expect

A large body of research shows that classroom methods that actively involve students result in substantially greater learning than pure lecturing does. Active learning methods may involve working in studio settings or on projects (e.g., McDermott and Redish, 1999), interactive lecture demonstrations (Sokoloff & Thornton, 1996), or peer discussions during lectures about conceptual questions—questions that probe the meaning of a subject, not just the ability to calculate. (See Appendix 3.) Clickers work particularly well with peer discussions, as described in Chapter 6.

Some of the clearest documentation of the success of more active teaching approaches can be found in physics, as the field of physics education research has been active for many years. An important aspect of that field is the existence of several testing instruments such as the *Force Concept Inventory* (Hestenes et al., 1992), which, even though they are multiple-choice tests, are generally agreed to be good probes of students' conceptual understanding. Such instruments are generally developed through research, often on the basis of interviews with many students, that identifies students' most common misconceptions. The misconceptions are then used to create the "distractors," or wrong answers, on the tests. Such tests work remarkably well in identifying whether students have learned important concepts, and the tests can be given to large numbers of students.

Hake (1998) used the Force Concept Inventory (FCI) to survey the learning gains of 6,000 students in 62 physics classes at a number of learning institutions. Since students often start with different levels of knowledge, results are reported as normalized learning gains. A "normalized gain" is the fraction of possible improvement a student achieves. For example, a student who scores 40% correct on the FCI the first week of a class could possibly improve 60% during the term. If the student achieves 70% when retaking the FCI at the end of the term, the normalized gain, < g >, is 30% improvement/60% possible improvement = 0.5. A key result from Hake's paper is shown here, where T marks the courses taught with traditional lectures and IE marks the courses taught with interactive educational methods.

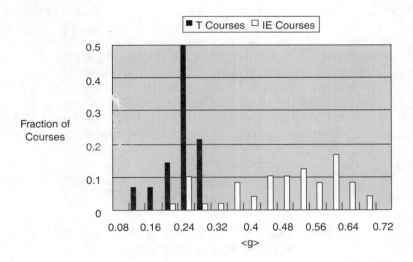

This graph shows that even the best traditional lecture courses produced only about a quarter of the possible learning gains. Furthermore, the difference between excellent lecturers and poor ones was surprisingly small. Even the worst of the more interactive classes did better than most of the lecture classes. Hake also found that the worst interactive results all came from classes where the instructor was not well-trained in interactive methods or where there were serious equipment problems. These results certainly encourage clicker use and argue strongly for introducing at least some active methods into lecture classes.

Just using clickers in class does not mean that your class will immediately achieve the results of an interactive education course. But clickers are especially well adapted for use in peer instruction, an interactive technique that is easy to start with just a small number of peer discussion questions, as described in Chapters 6 and 7. However, the best peer instruction carefully integrates into the overall curriculum the conceptual questions students are asked to discuss and answer. Furthermore, as mentioned in Appendix 3, midterm and final exams are designed to test conceptual knowledge. Our advice is to start with a limited number of clicker questions, evaluate how happy *you* are with the results, and proceed from there.

Attitude Gains You Can Expect

Although the main goal of instructors is for students to learn, student attitudes toward your subject should not be ignored. If we truly believe that learning is a lifelong process, we will be happier with a student who leaves a course thinking the subject matter was interesting and involving rather than one who leaves thinking it was irrelevant and boring. Appendix 2 presents a compendium of the comments of students in a large lecture course when peer discussion was introduced. Because the course was taught for 4 years before clickers were available, the comments were engendered by peer instruction, not clicker use. It is clear that these nonscience majors found peer discussion involving and interesting, and equally clear that previously they had not felt that way about science classes.

At the University of Massachusetts, students were directly asked how clicker use affected their class enjoyment. Typical results for a class of several hundred follow.

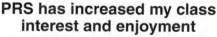

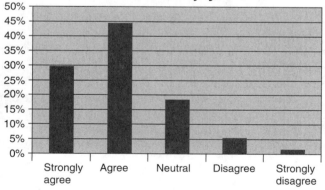

Instructors' Opinions about Using Clickers

Most instructors are enthusiastic about using clickers and feel that some practice makes the experience better. The following typical verbatim comments are from the survey of Trees and Jackson (2003):

"Better attendance, less sleeping in class, more background noise because they get in the habit of talking in class during clicker questions."

"I love what clickers have done for my classroom. The main benefits are (1) increased attendance; (2) active participation; (3) better preparation for class."

"Compared to . . . conventional lectures it's a world of difference—more engagement, better feedback in both directions, makes large classes feel much smaller."

"Students did seem really interested in seeing how the questions were answered by their classmates. They would react when they saw the graph."

How Classroom Response Systems Work, How to Register One, and How to Deal with Common Problems

Key Points

- Using clickers
- Getting a discount
- Registering clickers
- Dealing with technical problems
- Asking questions
- Grading student responses
- Finding recommended manufacturers and more information

Using Clickers

Here's how a typical clicker system works. Each student has a transmitter (or a remote; we call it a "clicker" in this book) that looks very much like a small TV remote control. A clicker is battery-powered, and each has a number of buttons, for instance, a, b, c, d, and e or the digits 1–9, and sometimes an extra button or two. Pushing a button transmits an infrared signal.

Two examples of clickers.

The classroom has one or more receivers that pick up the signals generated when a student pushes one of the buttons, and a computer equipped with appropriate software, provided by the clicker manufacturer, records each student's response. Usually an LCD projector is attached to the computer to display results to the class, usually without student names attached and typically as a bar chart showing how many students answered a, b, c, d, and e.

Students usually purchase clickers at a campus bookstore. Prices originally were about $30 but by the summer of 2004 were falling rapidly. Students may use their clickers in more than one class.

The classroom or lecture hall is wired with receivers located around the room. Receivers have a response time of about 0.1 to 0.01 second, depending on brand and model, which means that for votes to be recorded quickly, you need one receiver for every 25–40 students. If two students point at the same receiver at the same time, only one student will have his or her response detected. Faster receivers are a big help in preventing "jams" like this, as is instructing your students not to point at the same receiver, if there is more than one. (In a large lecture hall there will be many receivers.)

A classroom also needs a PC to run the data-collecting software and, usually, an LCD projector to display the vote results. Many instructors prefer to use a separate projector (or overhead projector, etc.) to display their questions. You will probably already have something similar that you use for course content. As explained below, you need to display a clicker status screen continuously while students are answering your question, so two projectors are very useful.

To use the student response system, the instructor projects the question and multiple-choice answers in front of the class. If this is done with a separate projector, you can do it any way you like. How you compose your questions is not a big deal. You can use your preferred software, such as MS-Word or PowerPoint, or simply write questions by hand. The latter is especially useful if you think of a new question to ask students during classtime. Data-collecting software from the major clicker companies (provided for free) allows you to import questions and show them on the same screen used to display the student data. If you choose to do this, you can use software such as PowerPoint or Blackboard to write questions that can then be imported into the data-collecting program. In fact, the data-recording system doesn't necessarily record the questions, just the answers. So whether you keep your questions separate or integrate them is up to you.

Sample Question

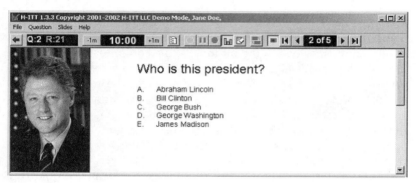

A sample question screen

During the voting period, a status screen is displayed that indicates which students' votes have been received so far. The screen shows a matrix in which each element corresponds to an individual student, and the cells contain the last few digits of the clicker ID. (In some systems the screens can be set to display the students' initials.) Cells always have the same color and position in the matrix throughout the semester, so students can learn which box represents them. This positioning is established the first time clickers are used in class. When a student sees her cell appear, she knows for certain that her vote has been recorded.

Data-Collection Screen

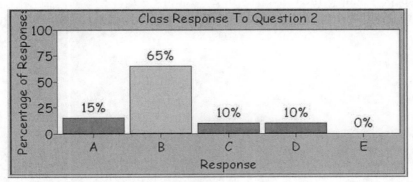

High Speed! H-ITT 1.4.5 Copyright 2001-2004 H-ITT LLC Biology 101 Section 1, Me										_ □ ✕

File Question Slides Help

← **Q:3 R:123** -1m **09:43** +1m

000			010	025			028		022	005
		029	015		024	017			004	021
018		020	023						012	006
067		107			086	031	148			069
098	097		135	140	136		132	087		
192		074			055	128	170	158		
	113	126		174	051	165	089	060		197
191	120	053	109	142	156					080
	133	152	193	181	057	194	045	144		
		071		127	118				166	034
	155	161	033	117		139			185	078
	115		079	105	104			046	177	076
	183	172	196	110		159				050
171			198	137	081			116		041
	070	083			134	188	044	180	163	
147		091				064			056	
190		149	037			043				058
168	100	146		106	173	096				
119				093	065	141	121			
		182	082	122	054	111	090			

The data-collection screen allows students to see whether their answers have been recorded, shows the elapsed time at the top, etc. It would be typical to give a warning such as, "20 seconds left. . ." and then stop the voting. The instructor then sees, and optionally projects, the results.

When everyone has voted, the instructor closes the vote and has the option of showing the class a histogram of the results.

Results Histogram

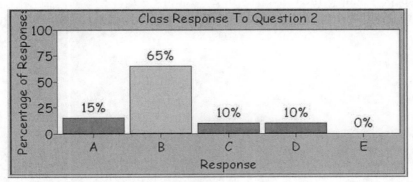

This screen shows the results. Grading of student votes is done separately with another program. It is possible to change how you grade answers at any later time.

Getting a Discount

Many textbook manufacturers have discount arrangements with clicker manufacturers, and instructors can ask about this when they order their textbooks. See your Addison-Wesley/Benjamin-Cummings sales representative
for more details on what is available to you, your department, and your students. Some manufacturers even give away receivers. If a campus store
orders, say, 500 clickers, a school will receive a certain number of free
receivers. These discounts are worth investigating.

Registering Clickers

If you want to use clickers merely to get survey information, they do not
need to be registered. However, most instructors want to associate particular answers with the students who gave them, in order to give the students
credit. In that case, students must register their clickers so that each clicker ID, the unique number stamped on each one, is associated with a particular student name.

Registration can be done via e-mail; software systems typically have a
program that automatically reads e-mail registration information if it is written in a specified format. Many instructors are familiar with class management software such as WebCT, and it is possible to set up registration
through such systems. Students can also register by hand—by filling out a
list in class that you type in later. Registration can be done at a local Web
site as well.

Web Site Registration

An example of Web site registration is shown on the next page (from the
physics department at the University of Colorado).

Please fill out this form to register your clicker

Class:	None ▾
First Name (No spaces)	
Last Name (No spaces)	
9 digit Student ID (No spaces or dashes)	
Re-Enter your Student ID:	
Numerical Clicker ID (No spaces or dashes) Look under the battery cover. Enter the numbers only, not leading letters.	
Re-Enter your Clicker ID:	
Your email Address: Only .colorado.edu emails are permitted	

REGISTER

This Web site produces a list of students and their clicker IDs in a format suitable for use with the software from the clicker company (usually a simple comma-separated value format). Notice that students are asked to enter their student ID and clicker ID twice. It is very important that students register their clickers carefully! If either number is off, even by one digit, students will get no credit for their answers.

Encourage students to register their clickers the first few days of class. In our experience, in a class of several hundred students, it is not unusual for several students to approach the instructor weeks into class and say, "Your system isn't giving me credit for my clicker answers." Tracking down incorrectly registered clickers can be time-consuming, so it is important that the clickers are registered correctly right from the start.

At the beginning of the term, ask your students some warm-up questions that do not count for a grade, to get them used to using their clickers and to find out if anyone has not been correctly registered. Try and make even these questions interesting and thought-provoking so that right from the start students associate clicker use with careful thinking rather than a game show.

Dealing with Technical Problems

One problem that may occur is clicker failure. The failure rate for most clickers has decreased and is now perhaps a few percent per semester. Nevertheless this means that you can still expect a handful of failures.

Companies are good at replacing bad clickers at no cost, but when a student registers the new clicker, the association of student ID and clicker will change. You may need to be prepared to handle that.

There may also be times when a student simply fails to bring his clicker to class. Policy on this varies from instructor to instructor. Some accept a small number of submissions on paper, and enter them later. Another common strategy is to tell students that a certain number (e.g., 4–8) of their lowest-scoring clicker answers will be dropped from their final grades. Such a policy saves a lot of time that otherwise would be spent dealing with student requests for makeup work.

Asking Questions

As described above, how you project questions and multiple-choice answers is very much up to you. Most instructors like the flexibility of having two projectors, one for their questions and one for the data-collection screen. The projector used for regular presentation to the class (LCD, overhead, etc.) is simply used to project the question and possible answers. When a question is asked, the data-collection screen is projected off to the side. Or, as described previously, questions can be merged in such a way that only one screen is used. For more detail, see the descriptions that major manufacturers put online.

After a while you probably will get used to being able to measure what your students are thinking, and then it will not be uncommon to suddenly think of a question you'd like to ask them during a class you are running (not "lecturing," because as you will see in a later chapter, the greatest power of clickers is in making a classroom more interactive, and you may be doing less lecturing than before). In any case, it is perfectly possible to think up a question and, say, write it on an overhead projector and ask for student responses. In that case, though, you must not forget to record the question you asked, because the data-collection system will record your students' answers but not your question!

If you have a teaching or other assistant, you may wish to make that person responsible for operation of the data-collection software, especially if you are using two screens. This can be a particular help when you are learning the system. Opinions vary widely about how difficult it is to manage two screens, but a majority of faculty members seem to have no trouble after they are used to the system. The author finds it extremely valuable to circulate through the room while students are answering questions and to listen to the discussions they are having with each other (when peer discussions are encouraged, as described in Chapter 6). In that case it is convenient, though not necessary, to have an assistant stop the data-collection software.

Plan on an extra 5 minutes prior to the start of each class to set up and test the system. The software is mostly intuitive, but it is also powerful and flexible and takes a few days to get thoroughly used to. Dealing with occasional student complaints or lost or forgotten clickers also takes some time. Again, during the first class you use clickers, try a few simple, noncredit questions to allow students to find out if their clickers are working and for you to determine if everyone is registered correctly.

Technically, then, it is not difficult to ask questions. *Pedagogically*, the composition of good, thought-provoking questions has never been easy and has always been a key part of teaching science. Some uses of clickers, for instance, to determine if students have done preclass reading, call for matter-of-fact questions. That use is straightforward. A clicker system also automatically records attendance, another straightforward use (but see Chapter 10 on cheating). Presumably, though, one of your main motivations in using clickers is to enhance student learning of, involvement in, and enjoyment of science. To promote this, good questions are required. An approach that lets students discuss answers with each other before answering has proven powerful and successful. It is discussed in detail in Chapter 6, "Clickers and Cooperative or Peer Instruction." For now, consider the more basic point that bad questions include ones that are too easy, or too hard. (See Appendix 3.) It is OK to start with some easy questions, but constant use of simple questions will bore your students. They are likely to be less impressed with the clicker technology than you are. In fact, many will start out not liking the use of clickers for reasons discussed in the next chapter, "How Clickers Will Change Your Classroom—A Warning!" You will need to address those concerns, in ways that chapter suggests.

Questions that result in a variety of answers on the response histogram are generally the most useful. They indicate that students have a variety of opinions (or a variety of confusions) and that a teaching opportunity is at hand.

Grading Student Responses

Any grading of student responses is done separately, not as a part of data collection. As the instructor, you will use data-analysis software that assigns whatever values you specify for specific answers. If a correct answer is "c," you might assign 1 point for that answer and 0 for any other. However, many instructors prefer to give partial credit for wrong answers. We give 2 points for wrong answers and 3 points for the correct one. Why? Because our questions are difficult, conceptual ones, and one of our main class goals is to encourage more student participation in science discussions. When students realize they get substantial credit for contributing, they are less afraid to give a "wrong" answer. See Chapter 8 for a more extensive discussion of grading.

Finding Recommended Manufacturers and More Information

The classroom response systems currently in use at universities across the country include H-ITT, or Hyper-Interactive Teaching Technology, *http://www.h-itt.com*, EduCue, *http://www.EduCue.com*, and eInstruction, *http://www.einstruction.com* (sometimes referred to by the name of their system, "CPS," or classroom performance system). All of these are one-way systems that transmit infrared signals. "One-way" means that students transmit a signal to the receiver; it does not transmit back. As described above, students need to check their transmitter's serial number on the screen to be sure their answer has been recorded.

A second type of classroom response system is "two-way," in which the receiver also transmits to the student, confirming the vote has been recorded. These systems often transmit radio (rf) rather than infrared signals. They also have a longer range and are more expensive. The leading rf manufacturer is Reply (the Fleetwood Group, *http://www.replysystems.com*). In the spring of 2004, eInstruction announced a two-way rf system as well. In situations where it is essential to confirm that all answers have been recorded (e.g., in the administration of high-stakes tests or exams), a two-way system has obvious advantages over a one-way system in that it eliminates the need for students to watch that their answers have been recorded. In spring 2004, two-way systems were much more expensive than one-way ones.

Although most instructors report that the software that comes with response systems is relatively convenient to use and easy to learn, a significant minority disagree, and this opinion varies from system to system. It may be worth your while to download the software from a manufacturer before buying in order to evaluate it for yourself. The University of Colorado's choice of which system to purchase was influenced by ease of use of the software.

Hardware problems have occasionally been reported. One major manufacturer apparently produced a batch of clickers with flaws that made it difficult to register student responses, causing so much frustration and anxiety among students that some faculty members stopped using the system. We have heard of only one such large-scale report of trouble, so hardware problems seem to be rare.

4

How Clickers Will Change Your Classroom— A Warning!

Key Points

- Clickers contradict student expectations
- Explaining why clickers are being used
- What it means to *really* learn science

Clickers Contradict Student Expectations

Classroom response systems are relatively easy to set up and use. This can lead you to think that if you just set one up and use it, all will be fine. Not so fast . . . ! While clicker technology is simple, its effects on the classroom are complex and can be challenging to manage. Think about things from students' points of view. Especially in a large university class, students have certain expectations: They will be relatively anonymous; they should sit up front and sometimes raise their hands if they want to be noticed; they should sit in the back of the lecture hall if they want to catch up on homework or read a newspaper; if a lecture doesn't seem that it will be worthwhile, they should just stay home—no one will notice, and they aren't graded just for showing up in class.

The use of a clicker system shatters these student expectations. For that reason, it is *critical* to explain during the first class meetings why clickers are being used and what the students will gain from their use. They also may be nervous when they realize that you can "test" them at any time, and that the clicker system can be used to show who attends class and who doesn't.

Explaining Why Clickers Are Being Used

Explain to your students that:

- Active learning lasts longer than passive listening.
- When they answer questions, they remember the answers better than if you just tell the answers to them.
- They will remember answers even better when they discuss questions with each other before answering. (See Chapter 6.)
- Proper clicker use can lead to higher grades.
- You will give some credit just for participation and they need not obsess over their clicker grades.
- Clicker questions allow you to find out whether they understand without their having to raise their hands.
- Many students think that using clickers is a lot of fun!
- They can e-mail you with any questions.

What It Means to *Really* Learn Science

In fact, if you use clickers with conceptual questions (see Chapter 6), you will be breaking an even more fundamental student expectation—what it means to learn. Many students believe that learning is the process of sitting in class, taking notes, memorizing them, and using the ideas from the notes to solve essentially similar problems on an exam a few weeks in the future. They may be surprised, disappointed, and frustrated if you ask them to apply the scientific concepts you've taught them to solve different-looking problems based on the same concepts. You may be surprised, disappointed, and frustrated to find they cannot *apply* what they've supposedly learned. This is the kind of realization that led Halloun and Hestines (1985), Eric Mazur (1997), and others to discover and document how students can appear to learn from lectures when, in fact, they have not reached a very deep level of understanding. Clickers, used with conceptual questions, cause students to confront their misconceptions immediately, rather than weeks later on a test. Students may complain, "This is hard." Indeed, deep learning of science is not easy. Again, the best strategy is to talk about this with them explicitly.

Studies have shown that for students in physics courses, their "epistemo-logical" beliefs—their views about the nature of knowledge and learning—

affect how they approach the courses. A student who believes that physics knowledge consists primarily of disconnected facts and formulas will study differently from a student who views physics as an interconnected web of concepts. The latter view leads to deeper and more long-lasting learning, but it indeed takes more work and more careful thinking. It is worth discussing this expectation with your students. Teachers interested in delving into these issues more deeply should look at Elby (2001).

As described elsewhere in this book, the use of clickers almost always raises class attendance. A few instructors who've taught required classes have reported that students who, before clickers were used, would not have attended class were now attending (and disrupting) class. To quote one instructor,

> Of course, any time a group is larger, it is likely to be louder. However, the students who were now attending classes for the "clicker points" were students who otherwise would not attend. Many of these students were seniors taking this entry-level course out of sequence. These students were often inattentive or disruptive in class, and would resent feeling that they had to attend or risk "losing points," even when the points were extra credit. For some class periods the additional noise was high enough that I had to stop and wait for the class to quiet down before continuing. Student reports suggest this then had the additional unintended consequence of frustrating the students who did want to come to class and who were attentive.

However, this instructor was using clickers for the first time, and had not discussed with the class the reasons for clicker use.

Student anxiety about the technology can also be a significant problem with clickers. For many students, this is the first time they have had their grades depend on a piece of equipment. The more students worry about whether their answers are being captured, the less they will be able to concentrate on learning. Giving students regular feedback about their clicker results is a good strategy for reducing anxiety. Doing that and repeating the benefits of clicker use several times during the term are both recommended.

5

What Are Your Class Goals and How Can Clickers Help Achieve Them?

Key Points

- Being clear with your goals
- Asking factual questions
- Asking conceptual questions
- Asking thought-provoking questions
- Increasing students' enthusiasm
- Increasing class attendance

Being Clear with Your Goals

Clickers are good for many things. If you want to ascertain whether students have done the assigned reading, for instance, at the start of class ask one or two straightforward questions based on the reading. You may want to sample student attitudes, or assess what they know about a topic before you teach it. The important thing is to be clear about your goals, and to ask questions *that support your goals!* As Tobias and Raphael (1997) report in *The Hidden Curriculum,* there is often a mismatch between what professors say they value, and what they test for.

A survey conducted by the American Astronomical Society found that only half the faculty who teach introductory astronomy had ever written down their goals. Presumably this is because "Everybody knows what's in the introductory course." Try it. Write down your goals and look at them.

Don't forget attitudinal or affective goals. When faculty members actually write down their goals, they are often surprised to find that some of what they are teaching and testing for does not, in fact, support their aims. You then may drop some topics or reduce their priority, giving time for more thorough discussion of more important topics.

Asking Factual Questions

Mismatch often occurs when instructors value conceptual understanding but test primarily for facts. Bloom (1956) and successors have postulated that cognition operates on ascending levels of complexity. A person begins with knowledge, or informational details, and moves upward through comprehension, analysis, and synthesis to evaluation. Asking factual questions is easy with clickers, but responses of factual knowledge don't necessarily indicate conceptual understanding. Consider this example that has been passed around in learning circles for many years:

> The Monotillation of Traxoline (Attributed to Judy Lanier)
> It is very important that you learn about traxoline. Traxoline is a new form of zionter. It is montilled in Ceristanna. The Ceristannians gristerlate large amounts of fevon and then bracter it to quasel traxoline. Traxoline may well be one of our most lukized snezlaus in the future because of our zionter lescelidge.
> Answer the following questions . . . .
>
> 1. What is traxoline?
> 2. Where is traxoline montilled?
> 3. How is traxoline quaselled?
> 4. Why is it important to know about traxoline?

Not much depth of knowledge is required to achieve a high score!

Asking Conceptual Questions

Just because clickers register only multiple-choice answers does not mean you can use them only for low-level (in Bloom's sense) fact-based questions. On the contrary, extensive research over the last 15 years has shown that conceptual questioning is possible even with multiple-choice questions. In physics this is powerfully demonstrated by the work of Hestenes et al. (e.g., 1992). Multiple-choice questions in which the wrong answers are based on common student misconceptions are a powerful way to test conceptual understanding. Sample conceptual questions and factual recall questions are given in Appendix 1.

If you try to teach more conceptual knowledge in class, by all means be sure to test for it in your exams! Students are often upset when there is a mismatch between what is taught in class and what is tested for in exams (cf. Tobias and Raphael, 1997).

Asking Thought-Provoking Questions

Higher-level questions that require evaluation may not have a unique correct answer but can strongly engage students, especially if you ask them to convince their neighbors. (See Chapter 6.) The clicker system can let students see the responses of others in the class, sometimes provoking further or more thoughtful discussion, which may be one of your goals. "Should we spend money searching for life elsewhere in the universe?" is an example of such a question in astronomy. "If you were a prospective parent, would you want to see the results of in vitro genetic testing?" might be asked in a biology class.

Increasing Students' Enthusiasm

Clicker use will probably increase the value students place on your lectures and increase class attendance. In a class of about 200 students taught first without clickers and later with them, Weiman and Perkins (2004) found that in the "clicker class," students rated the lectures significantly more useful to their learning than students in the nonclicker class did. The same is true of experiments and demonstrations done in science classes. When students were asked to *predict* experiment results before the experiment was done, they remembered and valued the experiments more (cf. Chapter 9).

A survey of 1,500 students in seven clicker classes across various subjects at the University of Colorado (Trees and Jackson, 2004) found a strong preference among students for getting feedback in large classes, and a strong agreement that they liked feeling engaged, two things that clickers can enhance. A majority reported that the clicker classes felt friendlier than nonclicker classes. However, a significant number expressed a preference for remaining anonymous in large classes and said the clickers made them feel "watched." The survey indicates that *students pay more serious attention to clicker questions in courses that are more heavily structured around clicker use or that involve discussion of clicker answers.* The survey also suggests that instructors who have used clickers before have slightly better results than those using them for the first time. More details are given in Chapter 9, "What Do Students Think of Using Clickers?"

Similar results were found at the University of Massachusetts. Students generally liked clicker use, and their ratings of professors who used clickers improved as the professors became more experienced.

Effectiveness Improves with Use

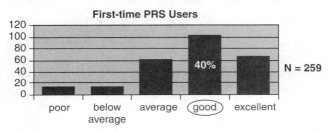

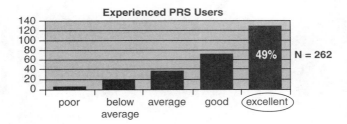

Clickers usually, though not always, help in generating student enthusiasm. Whether they do so apparently depends on how they are used, how their use is explained to students, and how clicker answers are graded. More research is needed here. When used with peer discussions (see Chapter 6), the affect on student attitudes is often positive.

Increasing Class Attendance

The Trees and Jackson survey (2003) found that about 80% of students reported that clicker points motivated them to come to class, whether the points were part of their regular class grade or extra credit. Almost all instructors using clickers report increased attendance. In large physics and astronomy classes at the University of Colorado, attendance is typically 80% or more throughout the semester. However, as mentioned in Chapter 4, some instructors report a downside to increased class attendance in that some of the students who used to skip class now attend but do so with a poor attitude that can be disruptive.

In summary, research and observation have shown that clickers are a powerful tool that can be used to help attain goals shared by many teachers. However, they are only a tool, and an instructor needs to have clear goals and a plan of how clickers can help address his or her goals for their use to be particularly effective. Furthermore, it is essential to articulate those goals to students before starting a class that will use clickers.

6

Clickers and Cooperative Learning or Peer Instruction

Key Points

- Significant and lasting learning
- Cooperative learning or peer instruction
- Clickers and peer instruction
- Students' cognitive gains
- Students' attitude gains

Significant and Lasting Learning

Educational studies have clearly shown that for significant and lasting learning to take place, students' minds must be active. When students take a new concept and relate it to what they already know, apply it to solve a problem, or explain it to another person, they are engaging in the sorts of activities that result in lasting understanding. Listening passively to a lecture, *even a good, clear one*, often fails to bring about the same results. Sometimes lectures may lead students to active thought and analysis, but this doesn't often happen. When taught by traditional means, students can often pass a test, but they may be unable to apply the same concepts in the real world. Furthermore, much of the knowledge they gain passes from their minds not long after the exam. One can be a good teacher whom students appreciate and the winner of many teaching awards and yet cause less lasting learning to take place than the teacher and students think. Many studies have also shown that if a student enters class with a misconception, a good, clear explanation of the correct answer often *fails* to displace the student's incorrect idea. Research has found that we must allow our students a chance to apply their own ideas because *only if these fail* are students likely to replace their previous concepts with ones we have taught them. Such findings present a clear challenge to those of us who teach science. For a dramatic and entertaining illustration of this, we recommend the remarkable videos *A Private Universe* and *Minds of Our Own* (see the References).

More effective ways of teaching science are known, such as in groups, in labs, and in studio or lecture-tutorial settings that are outside the scope of this book. But what can the instructor in a large lecture class do? A successful and relatively easy way to cause students to be more active is to engage them in peer or cooperative learning. Peer instruction has been developed and used by a number of people in different fields. Here we will describe the results achieved in physics by Eric Mazur and in astronomy by the author, and show how naturally clickers work with peer instruction.

Cooperative Learning or Peer Instruction

Peer instruction is based on two ideas:

1. Asking conceptual questions that probe students' understanding of a topic
2. Getting students to discuss/argue/debate and try to convince each other of the correct answer

Mazur has done this at Harvard since the early 1990s. We highly recommend his book *Peer Instruction: A User's Manual* (1997). The author experimented with peer learning in astronomy classes at the University of Chicago in the mid-1990s (Duncan, 1999). Assessment of his students' attitudes is summarized in Appendix 2. Both instructors now use clickers to facilitate peer instruction.

Clickers and Peer Instruction

Peer instruction calls for an instructor to probe student understanding whenever an important new concept is introduced, and after students have supposedly learned it. Conceptual clicker questions are ideally suited for this since they generally do not require any calculation. (See Appendix 3.) Here are two examples:

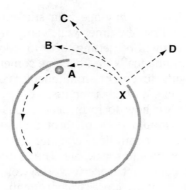

1. A marble is rolled around a circular piece of metal, as shown in the figure. The metal ends at X (the circle is not complete). When the ball gets to X, which path does it follow?
   a. A
   b. B
   c. C
   d. D
2. If you were on the moon, the earth would
   a. Show no phases
   b. Show phases that are the same as the moon's (when it is a full moon it is a full earth, etc.)
   c. Show phases opposite to the moon (when it is a full moon it is a new earth, etc.)

Many traditional astronomy textbooks never ask a question like number 2, but if you understand the cause of the phases of the moon, it is easy to figure out the phases of the earth as seen from the moon. If you don't understand the concept, there is nowhere to look up the answer!

A good conceptual clicker question results in about half of the class getting the correct answer. Mazur considers 40–80% a good range. If too few answer correctly, you need to explain further before proceeding, or students' discussions will falter. If almost all students understand the concept, you may choose to move on. Otherwise, you can proceed to step 2 of peer instruction.

Ask your students to turn to their left and right in the lecture hall, form a group of three, and convince each other which answer is correct. Tell them how many minutes they have (e.g., 2–3) and assure them that you will ask the clicker question again at the end of that time. *It is essential that you explained before trying this how you expect peer discussion to work.* As noted in Chapter 1, you will have to convince your students that you really want them to talk in class. The first few times will seem strange to them, but after that, your biggest problem will be getting them to stop. The ambience of the classroom will change dramatically and become something like a professional scientific meeting, with dozens of simultaneous conversations going on, some of which may become quite passionate.

Many variations exist on how to form peer discussion groups, including whether the same ones should be kept throughout the term, whether the male-female ratio should be controlled, whether roles should be assigned to be sure everyone gets a chance to speak, etc. The author strongly advises that you try the simple approach first since it works well, is easy, and takes no more of your time than a pure lecture, except for the need to prepare good questions.

Remember that for peer discussions to work well, the students need to have enough background information that about half of them will know the correct answer. Often this knowledge will come from before-class reading you have assigned. Clickers may be used at the start of class with relatively simple questions to check whether students have done the reading. The *conceptual questions* require deeper thinking, and when students work in groups, you will find that more of them are able to answer deeper questions. They really help each other learn.

What should you do while the students are talking? Circulate around the classroom and listen to what they are saying. It is very profitable and often surprising, to be able to sample student reasoning "in progress." They may ask you for interpretation or advice, which may cause you to make your questions clearer in the future.

Many instructors find that initially the most difficult part of peer instruction is saying nothing while the students are the ones doing lots of talking. Your role has changed from the "sage on the stage" to the "guide on the side" and it takes considerable self-confidence to move from the expert role to more of a provocateur role. It may help to remember that:

1. Asking questions was good enough for Socrates.
2. The data show that your students are likely to learn more (see below).
3. You will probably enjoy the enthusiasm generated in your class, especially if you have been teaching for some time.

Students' Cognitive Gains

In peer discussion students are being taught by nonexperts—other students. Will they learn as much as from listening to the instructor? Will the "wrong" students convince the "right" ones? One of the best data sets to examine such questions is from the physics course taught by Mazur at Harvard, since he has taught more than a decade both with and without peer instruction. Mazur was motivated to investigate his students' conceptual understanding by the work of Hestenes et al. (1992). Their Force Concept Inventory (FCI) is a research-based multiple-choice test in which the wrong answers are based on commonly held student misconceptions. The FCI is not easy. The gains of Mazur's students have been much greater in the years when peer instruction replaced part of the lecture. In fact, the gains shown in his first trial in 1991 were higher than the gains in *any* professor's pure lecture class. The results of subsequent years have been similar. The "threshold" indicated in the graphs below corresponds to what is generally considered mastery of the subject.

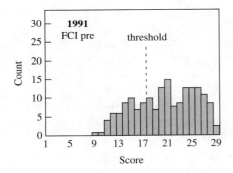 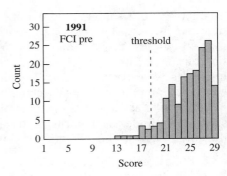

In the last year of the author's peer teaching at the University of Chicago, a survey instrument known as the Astronomy Diagnostic Test (Deeming, 2001) became available. Like the FCI, it is a difficult multiple-choice test with wrong answers based on misconceptions commonly held by students. Pre- and post-test results were, respectively, 38% correct and 67% correct, a large improvement compared to most introductory astronomy classes.

It is still not entirely clear why peer instruction works so well; much research remains to be done in this area. However, the concern about wrong students convincing right ones turns out not to be very significant. Tracking how student answers change due to discussion shows far more wrong-to-right transitions than right-to-wrong. After observing peer interactions for about 6 years, we suggest that one reason for their success is the strong peer pressure that college students feel. Certainly, most students behave as if the opinion of others in their group is more important than the instructor's. After all, we just give them their grades; but if their friends think they're dumb, that's much worse! This opinion hasn't been researched, but the learning gains speak for themselves. The comments of an insightful student seem relevant as well:

"Professor X is an excellent teacher, but it is obviously better to learn from another student who thinks more like me."

Another concern you may have is that in classes such as physics and chemistry where numbers are important, the emphasis on conceptual understanding might hurt students' ability to calculate. At least in Mazur's classes, this was not the case. He regave a 6-year-old exam from the days when he delivered straight lectures and emphasized calculations, not concepts, and the class using peer instruction did about 10% *better* on the exam that emphasized calculations.

Students' Attitude Gains

Chapter 9 reports student attitudes about the use of clickers. A majority "like" their use in class. Appendix 2 presents a more thorough examination of student attitudes in a science class for nonscience majors that used peer instruction but not clickers (which weren't yet available). In this class many of the questions were based on class demonstrations or experiments. They were conceptual, but also concrete—something the students could see.

Full results are reported in Appendix 2, but one result was the change in students' attitudes. A majority of the students stated at the start of class that they didn't like science. Frequently reported reasons included:

1. I'm a creative person, so I'd like to do something creative.
2. I like to do things that are involving, and that involve other people.

Peer discussions of questions that have unknown answers or of experiments that produce surprising results address both these supposed failings of science, and the peer approach proved very successful. At the end of the term, students were asked (anonymously) if their attitude toward science had changed in any way. During all 4 years, more than 80% of students said yes, and almost all attitude changes were positive.

In the Trees and Jackson survey of 1,500 students (2003), an overwhelming majority reported that clickers helped them learn. The strongest responses (about 4 or higher, on a scale where 1 equaled "completely disagree" and 5 equaled "strongly agree") included "Clicker questions helped me know how well I was learning the material," "Getting feedback on my ideas helps me learn better," and "Clicker questions encouraged me to be more engaged in the classroom process."

7

Clickers and Classroom Demonstrations

Key Points

- Using clickers to predict demonstration results
- Presenting demonstrations that have surprising results
- Conducting "real-time" demonstrations with clickers

Using Clickers to Predict Demonstration Results

Many teachers like to give demonstrations, but research has shown that demonstrations are often not as effective as teachers would like. Those who have seen the *Private Universe* (Schneps and Sadler, 1987) video will recall that the demonstration given by the teacher didn't have much long-term effect on most students' learning. Chapter 2 presents an example from Weiman (2004) in which most students did not remember how a violin works 15 minutes after they saw the demonstration (possibly indicating that they never understood or internalized what the demonstration showed).

For several years Mazur (2004) has been studying how well students remember demonstrations and has discovered that weeks or months later, a significant number of students will incorrectly remember the demonstration if it contradicted their preconceptions. Students are conditioned to listen to their teacher, rather than learning for themselves, from their own observations.

The author saw an example of preconceived notions affecting what people see at the world-famous History of Science Museum in Florence, Italy. A museum curator conducted an experiment for visitors using an inclined plane that belonged to Galileo, which he'd used to measure acceleration. However, the apparatus had not been set up correctly to demonstrate acceleration, as a sign said it was supposed to. Galileo lived before stopwatches, and to time his experiments he sang a song to himself with even beats. The inclined plane had movable bells that would ding when a ball rolling down the plane passed a bell. Knowing that falling bodies accelerate, Galileo had, as the sign said, set up the lower bells with greater and greater spacing so that the ding interval would be the same. But anyone who looked at the museum demonstration could see that the bells were evenly spaced. Therefore, when the curator performed the experiment, the bells went "ding," "ding," "ding-ding-ding" with ever increasing frequency; but when the curator asked, "Did you hear the even spacing of the dings?" every visitor nodded and moved on to the next exhibit. Expectation had prevailed over direct observation.

One way to make demonstrations more effective is to use clickers and ask students to predict what the demonstration will show before you perform it. After the experiment, explicitly ask the students to indicate:

a. The experiment agreed with my prediction.
b. The experiment did not agree with prediction.

Do not take points off if the result didn't match students' predictions because the point of having them make predictions is to get the students' minds active and get them to commit to a result and be clear with themselves whether their ideas are correct or need to be changed.

In the author's experience with nonscience majors at the University of Chicago, few students really believed at the start of a term that science is determined by experiment, instead believing that a good argument is how issues are decided. Further, most of the students usually believed that *their* ideas were right. With more future lawyers and writers in the class than future scientists, perhaps this was not surprising. A main class goal was for the students to understand the scientific method. As Richard Feynman once said, "Science is a way of trying not to fool yourself," and in science the role of prediction followed by testing through experimentation is key.

Presenting Demonstrations That Have Surprising Results

We often chose experiments with results that would be surprising to the students as the basis for peer discussions, which we followed by asking for student predictions. These questions were called "Challenges," and the name turned out to be appropriate because students came to see them as challenges rather than just something to do for another grade. Often we set up the experiment about 10 minutes before the end of one class and gave students 5 to 10 minutes to engage in peer discussion. However, we didn't collect the predictions until the start of the next class, giving students plenty of time outside of class to ponder the experiment. By the time we actually performed the experiment, students were quite anxious to find out the result. That the result was often surprising (and the students were not penalized for guessing incorrectly) led to some of the enthusiasm reported in Chapter 6 and Appendix 2. In a few cases, such as our demonstration of the famous Galileo experiment of dropping a heavy object and a lighter object to see which falls faster, some students actually performed the experiment before the second class by dropping various objects off a dormitory balcony, which fulfilled our secondary class goal of encouraging students to recognize science in their everyday lives, not just in science class.

So although clickers give immediate feedback, you may consider using them sometimes with peer discussions, which will allow students more time than usual to think and discuss a question. A more complete discussion of the "Challenges" is given in Appendix 2.

Conducting Real-Time Demonstrations with Clickers

Rogers (2003) at the University of Massachusetts has used clickers in a statistics class by having the students take data and use their clickers to contribute in real time to a combined total, in order to demonstrate various statistical concepts. For instance, students can be asked to toss coins and report the results.

STATS LIVE!
Take out a coin. I have some extras.

Make a spot in your notebook to record your results
from tossing the coin 4 times and recording your
outcome, H or T.

	Your Outcome
Write	
	Toss 1 H or T
down your	Toss 2 H or T
	Toss 3 H or T
results!	Toss 4 H or T

Let A = # of heads in the 4 tosses.
What values can it take on? 0, 1, 2, 3, 4

Students are asked to toss four coins.

At the top of the next page students are asked to predict the probability of various outcomes. The student predictions are given on the graph on the right.

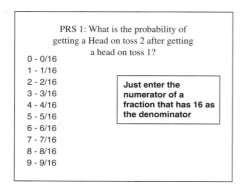

Students are asked to predict an outcome.

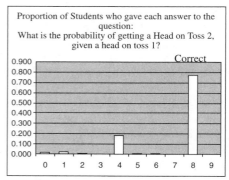

Student predictions

Approximately 20% of the students (those who answered 4/16) believe the so-called gambler's fallacy—that if you have tossed heads on toss 1, you are less likely to get heads on toss 2—rather than the correct odds of 50–50. As illustrated below, statistics lessons can be made more powerful by showing the students their own data. After flipping four coins, students enter their data with their clickers and then look at the combined class results:

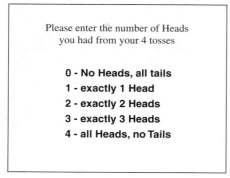

Instruction to the students

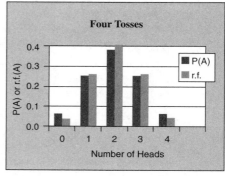

Results from all students (r.f.), compared with expectations (P(A))

Looking at the combined class data naturally leads to discussion of concepts such as sampling error, the importance of sample size, etc. Basic concepts of compiling and then analyzing data are important in many science classes, and the Rogers' approach is interesting to pursue. One could imagine demonstrating scientific concepts such as half-life and radioactive decay, random walk, and experimental error with real-time student input. The University of Massachusetts maintains an active discussion group concerning classroom response systems at http://www.umass.edu/cft/prs/.

8

To Grade or
Not to Grade?

Key Points

- Should you grade clicker responses?
- Stopping students from obsessing over grades

Should You Grade Clicker Responses?

Usually, you should grade clicker questions. Generally students expect to be rewarded for the work they do. Some instructors use clickers just to assess overall class knowledge before or after they introduce a subject. In some classes, a large box of clickers is available to the students, and students use them but do not own them, which eliminates both the need to register clickers and the problem of broken clickers.

Most faculty who have their students use clickers assign points for clicker answers. Think carefully about how you will assign points, and be sure your policy is aligned with your teaching goals. Many instructors have the goal of increasing students' class participation through clicker use. One way to do this is to give partial credit for wrong clicker answers. A correct answer might be worth 2 points and an incorrect answer 1 point. In classes for nonscience majors, some instructors even award 3 and 2 points, respectively. As discussed previously, introducing some provocative questions that don't have single correct answers can be very engaging to students. (Don't start with those types of questions, though.)

Stopping Students from Obsessing over Grades

The main problem instructors often encounter with giving clicker grades is that some students will obsess over them. (See Appendix 3.) Even if the clicker grade is a small percentage of the class grade, students may be very aware of it, perhaps because they see the clickers every class. Students may, in fact, become quite upset if they leave their clickers at home or if theirs breaks. (Keep in mind that a large percentage of "broken" clickers actually have batteries inserted incorrectly or dead batteries.) Be sure you formulate a policy for these situations before you encounter them. A common policy is to say at the start of the term that the lowest three or four clicker grades, including grades of 0, will be discarded. This allows students to miss a class or two, or have a broken clicker, without losing points.

Some instructors give only "bonus" points for clicker responses. Surprisingly perhaps, this does not seem to do much to lessen students' worry about their clicker grades. The best policy seems to be to make clickers a regular part of your class, with a use that's consistent with your goals, and to *explain early in the term and multiple times thereafter the benefits you expect clickers to bring to the students*.

To quote from one faculty member who has used clickers for several years, "Clickers account for 10% of their grade, with their lowest 20% of clicker days dropped. Students earn 50% clicker credit even if they give all wrong answers. Based on several semesters, I've learned that with no clickers, attendance drops to approximately 50% towards the end of semester; with 5% credit, attendance dips no lower than approximately 75%; and with 10% credit, attendance is 80–85%."

To quote another, "Clickers account for 10% of the grade. And they act like it's even more important than that!"

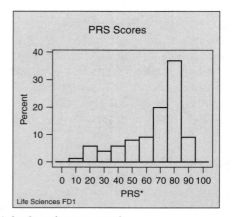

Determining the PRS Grade

- At each Lecture
  - [34 lectures; 41 less 1–5 days of term, and the 2 exam days]
- 2 to 8 Questions were asked
  - Some were ungraded survey questions to get data!
- Half credit for trying any answer
- Other half for being correct
- Each day was worth 2 points
- Dropped lowest 3 days [allows for "I forgot," absent, bad day...]
- Thus, if always present with clicker minimum PRS Score is 50%.

Life Sciences FD1

Sample of a clear grading policy and the scores it leads to (Rogers, 2003).

Showing students clicker scores from a previous semester or similar class can lessen anxiety. It can also demonstrate that most students will get good grades on their clicker use, and that using clickers will increase their learning and lead to better exam scores.

9

What Do Students Think of Using Clickers?

Key Points

- Finding out what students think of using clickers
- Dealing with students who don't like using clickers
- Students' tabulated opinions
- Students' verbatim opinions

Finding Out What Students Think of Using Clickers

Instructors can sample students' opinions of clicker use by asking them various questions: "Do you like using clickers?" "Do clickers help you learn?" "Do you prefer classes that use clickers to those that don't?" "What don't you like about using clickers?

Responses from a survey of 1,500 students in seven classes (five science, two communications) conducted by Trees and Jackson (2003) provide one set of answers to these questions. These and other survey results will be discussed in the pages that follow.

Dealing with Students Who Don't Like Using Clickers

Many instructors will overhear that students enjoy using clickers. For many students this is clearly true, as the quotations at the end of this chapter show. However, the more quantitative results in Table 9.1 remind us that there is a significant contingent of students who wish to remain anonymous in class and also prefer pure lectures. A good feature of clickers is that they allow students to get feedback while remaining relatively (more so than raising their hands) anonymous.

Table 9.1

Question	Average Answer
Getting feedback on my ideas helps me learn.	3.9
By using clickers I got feedback on my understanding.	3.6–4.4
If I had a choice I would avoid classes where the instructor just lectures.	3.25
The best way to teach large courses is with traditional lectures.	2.5
I prefer to remain anonymous in large classes.	3.25
In large classes I prefer to be involved and engaged.	3.0–3.6

The table uses a scale of 1 to 5, where 1 means "strongly disagree" and 5 means "strongly agree."

The averages reported here are only for the science classes. The communications classes were somewhat less successful with clicker use. This appears to be due to several factors including that clickers were new to the instructors teaching those classes and that clickers were less well integrated into the communications classes than in the science classes, which had been using clickers longer.

Some instructors would argue that students who prefer pure lectures are often the ones who *don't* want to be challenged and instead would prefer a class that allows them to pass merely by memorizing what the instructor says and feeding that information back on tests, rather than a class that requires them to demonstrate conceptual understanding or explain themselves to another student. How true this is goes beyond the scope of this book, but a revealing (and real) student quotation follows: "I expected that you would teach me. I didn't expect that I would have to learn!"

In any case we recommend that you are prepared to deal with a group of students who are not naturally inclined toward using clickers and all that their use involves. Carefully explain to your class the goals of your course and how clickers support those goals. Stress this early and then repeat it often during the term. Being sure that clickers work well technically and are well integrated into your teaching are also important factors in ensuring student satisfaction. A poorly implemented clicker system that experiences many technical failures is sure to sour the experience for many students.

Students' Tabulated Opinions

In Table 9.2 we see the wide variety of majors of the respondents to the Trees and Jackson survey.

Table 9.2

Major	N	% Response
Communications	288	18.9
Journalism	67	4.4
Arts	56	3.7
Humanities	57	3.7
Social Science	99	6.5
Natural Science	343	22.6
Engineering	209	13.7
Business	90	5.9
Architecture	90	5.8
Open Option/Undecided	222	14.6

Table 9.3 shows that students expected feedback to help their learning.

Table 9.3

Getting feedback on my ideas helps me learn better.

	Overall	ASTRO 1110-1	ASTRO 1110-2	ASTRO 1120	COMM 1210	COMM 1300	PHYS 1110	PHYS 2010
Mean	3.78	3.77	3.79	3.91	3.40	3.51	4.15	3.84
SD	.97	.96	.95	.88	1.04	.98	.78	.95

(On a scale of 1 to 5, where 1 means "strongly disagree" and 5 means "strongly agree.")

We see in Tables 9.4a–c that students' expectations for involvement in a large class differed from that for a small class.

Table 9.4a
I prefer to be anonymous in large classes.

	Overall	ASTRO 1110-1	ASTRO 1110-2	ASTRO 1120	COMM 1210	COMM 1300	PHYS 1110	PHYS 2010
Mean	3.26	3.50	3.25	3.09	3.38	3.10	3.04	3.33
SD	1.19	1.13	1.25	1.20	1.23	1.12	1.17	1.17

Table 9.4b
In large classes, I prefer to be involved and engaged.

	Overall	ASTRO 1110-1	ASTRO 1110-2	ASTRO 1120	COMM 1210	COMM 1300	PHYS 1110	PHYS 2010
Mean	3.19	3.01	3.02	3.04	2.58	2.85	3.69	3.58
SD	1.19	1.27	1.15	1.04	1.18	1.09	1.03	1.06

Table 9.4c
In small classes, I prefer to be involved and engaged.

	Overall	ASTRO 1110-1	ASTRO 1110-2	ASTRO 1120	COMM 1210	COMM 1300	PHYS 1110	PHYS 2010
Mean	4.04	4.00	3.80	4.15	4.14	3.98	4.08	4.05
SD	1.01	1.04	1.09	.87	1.04	.99	.99	.96

(On a scale of 1 to 5, where 1 means "strongly disagree" and 5 means "strongly agree.")

In examining what actually happened, as illustrated below in Tables 9.5a–c, it is important to note that instructors who were experienced using clickers taught the physics and astronomy classes. The communications classes were taught by instructors who were using clickers for the first time. The physics instructors had worked particularly hard to integrate clicker use into their curriculum.

There is a substantial variation in how helpful students found the clickers to be. *When clickers were well-integrated into the classroom, they were found to be extremely helpful.*

Table 9.5a
By using clickers in this class, I got feedback on my understanding of class material.

	Overall	ASTRO 1110-1	ASTRO 1110-2	ASTRO 1120	COMM 1210	COMM 1300	PHYS 1110	PHYS 2010
Mean	3.62	3.99	3.69	3.55	2.46	2.85	4.43	3.92
SD	1.26	1.02	.99	1.17	1.19	1.24	.80	1.06

Table 9.5b
Clicker questions helped me to know how well I was learning the material.

	Overall	ASTRO 1110-1	ASTRO 1110-2	ASTRO 1120	COMM 1210	COMM 1300	PHYS 1110	PHYS 2010
Mean	3.57	3.88	3.70	3.48	2.60	2.86	4.30	3.79
SD	1.23	1.04	.98	1.13	1.17	1.19	.83	1.17

Table 9.5c
Clicker questions were helpful for preparing me for the exams in class.

	Overall	ASTRO 1110-1	ASTRO 1110-2	ASTRO 1120	COMM 1210	COMM 1300	PHYS 1110	PHYS 2010
Mean	3.27	3.66	3.24	2.81	2.29	2.63	4.02	3.50
SD	1.29	1.20	1.14	1.13	1.15	1.17	.95	1.22

(On a scale of 1 to 5, where 1 means "strongly disagree" and 5 means "strongly agree.")

If clickers are to help learning, students must be serious about their use. A worry of some faculty is that since clickers operate a lot like a TV remote control, students might use them in a superficial way. The Trees and Jackson study asked several questions about this and about whether students thought they profited from interacting with their peers. See Tables 9.6a–c for the results.

Table 9.6a
I chose my answer to each clicker question carefully.

	Overall	ASTRO 1110-1	ASTRO 1110-2	ASTRO 1120	COMM 1210	COMM 1300	PHYS 1110	PHYS 2010
Mean	3.85	4.35	4.04	4.21	2.96	3.38	4.14	4.09
SD	1.08	.79	.94	.87	1.19	1.10	.82	.95

Table 9.6b
I pay attention to whether or not my answer to a clicker question was
  right or wrong.

	Overall	ASTRO 1110-1	ASTRO 1110-2	ASTRO 1120	COMM 1210	COMM 1300	PHYS 1110	PHYS 2010
Mean	4.34	4.59	4.45	4.60	3.70	3.92	4.61	4.56
SD	.98	.83	.94	.53	1.14	1.07	.80	.75

Table 9.6c
I'm learning more from my peers in this class than I do in other large
  classes.

	Overall	ASTRO 1110-1	ASTRO 1110-2	ASTRO 1120	COMM 1210	COMM 1300	PHYS 1110	PHYS 2010
Mean	3.13	3.30	2.95	3.09	2.19	2.38	3.59	3.83
SD	1.28	1.15	1.21	1.17	1.08	1.02	1.11	1.12

(On a scale of 1 to 5, where 1 means "strongly disagree" and 5 means "strongly agree.")

As shown in Tables 9.7a and 9.7b, the survey also confirmed what almost
all faculty members have observed: Clicker use increases class attendance:

Table 9.7a
For me, earning "clicker" points motivates me to come to class.

	Overall	ASTRO 1110-1	ASTRO 1110-2	ASTRO 1120	COMM 1210	COMM 1300	PHYS 1110	PHYS 2010
Mean	3.96	4.29	4.17	3.83	3.23	3.46	4.08	4.42
SD	1.23	.99	1.05	1.30	1.41	1.36	1.12	.92

Table 9.7b
I attended class when I otherwise would not have because of the
  clickers.

	Overall	ASTRO 1110-1	ASTRO 1110-2	ASTRO 1120	COMM 1210	COMM 1300	PHYS 1110	PHYS 2010
Mean	3.32	3.59	3.32	2.96	3.27	3.12	3.16	3.54
SD	1.38	1.30	1.35	1.32	1.37	1.36	1.39	1.40

(On a scale of 1 to 5, where 1 means "strongly disagree" and 5 means "strongly agree.")

Additional information on student responses to clickers is available from the University of Massachusetts at Amherst where clickers have been in use for a number of years (Rodgers, 2003).

Overall students there like clicker use very much. Over the last 5 years:

- 90% call clicker use a success
- 10% call it a failure

What they like:

- Instant feedback
- Break up lecture
- Opportunity to participate in lecture

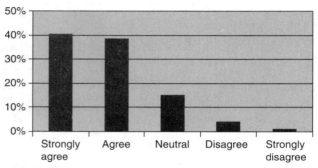

My experience has been positive and I encourage you to keep PRS

Student responses at University of Massachusetts, Amherst

How students at the University of Massachusetts view clickers and *why* they like them varies:

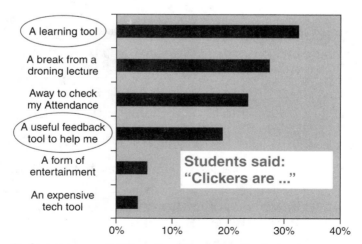

Student responses at University of Massachusetts, Amherst

Students' Verbatim Opinions

A majority of students report they enjoy using clickers, as shown in the graph in Chapter 2. However, not all do. Here are some typical, verbatim student comments.

Positive comments:

"It's fun as hell. Helps me learn and gives me confidence when I'm right!"

"It gives us, the students, an anonymous way of giving feedback to the teacher."

"It's easy and prepares you for exam-like questions."

"It gives us credit for coming to class (. . .)."

Negative comments:

"The PRS questions are too easy—I don't think it's worth the money."

"We do not have enough time to find the answers."

"It's far too expensive! When already paying $100 for a book, another $40 is a big deal."

"Sometimes you can't tell if your answer went through."

The negative comment about cost should soon be mitigated by falling prices. (See your Addison-Wesley/Benjamin Cummings sales representative for the latest offers.)

10

Clickers and Cheating

Key Points

- How often do students cheat?
- Preventing students from cheating

How Often Do Students Cheat?

Like most technologies, you can cheat with clickers. The most straightforward way is for one student to give his or her clicker to another (and possibly not attend the class at all). A survey of 1,500 University of Colorado students asked whether they had ever seen other students use more than one clicker during class. The percentage that said yes ranged from a low of 17% to a high of over 50%. Note that the question asked whether the students had ever seen the questionable behavior, anytime during the semester. Regular cheating was reported to be much lower.

The 17% figure is from the author's class, which was somewhat different in an important way: Unlike the other classes, it had small-group discussions led by undergraduates who had taken the class the previous term, as part of an NSF-funded project designed to expose more students to a possible career as a kindergarten to 12th grade science teacher. The fact that students in the large lecture could expect to be recognized by their discussion leader may have drastically reduced cheating. In other classes the percentage of observed cheating was higher. Again, the question asked whether cheating was ever observed; the actual amount of cheating is probably much lower.

Preventing Students from Cheating

It is important to discuss cheating right at the start of a class, when you discuss your expectations for clicker use. Emphasize that giving someone else your clicker is just like letting someone else take a quiz or exam for you, which in most schools can result in failure or worse. If appropriate, you might emphasize that the clicker points represent only a small part of students' grades and that cheating is pretty unwise in that it hinders one's learning. State that one of the things students in previous classes have liked most about clickers is the feedback they give them about what they understand and what they need to study more, and students feel this improves their overall performance and exam grades. Tell them that letting someone else use their clicker robs them of that feedback.

A Checklist—
Are You Ready?

Before starting a class using clickers, you should . . .

1. **Set up the classroom.**
   - Set up the clicker receivers, a computer, and acquisition software for receiving student input.
   - Set up a way of projecting questions and the student responses, and test it to see that it works.
   - Time yourself to find out how much set-up time you require before class.

2. **Test clickers in your classroom.**
   - Start the software and walk around the room with a clicker, testing its range to make sure there are no "blind spots."
   - Be sure all your trials got recorded. (Most systems have a "demo" mode that allows you to use the system even without registering students.)

3. **Test the registration system you intend to use.**
   - Pretend that you are a student and attempt to register your clicker. Register correctly and be sure the system works.
   - Deliberately make some mistakes while registering and see what happens.
   - Download into the clicker software the list of student names from registration. Did you end up with all the names you expected?

4. **Plan how you will grade clicker use (Chapter 8).**
   - Remember that students might obsess over clicker grades, so consider your goal in using clickers.
   - If your goal is to engage students actively in the material, make the clicker grade a small part of the class grade, give partial credit for

wrong answers, and use the techniques of peer instruction (Chapter 6).

- Make your grading policy clear in your syllabus.

5. **Compile a sufficient number of good clicker questions.**
   - Make up a few noncredit "icebreaker" questions to use in a non-graded way to let students practice clicker use in your first classes. You might consider surveying your students about their expectations for the class.
   - Decide on what mix of simple recall versus conceptual questions you want to ask.
   - Come up with good questions for use during the term.
   - Ask your textbook publisher if they have predeveloped, pretested CRS questions.
   - Share good questions with your colleagues.

6. **In your first class . . .**
   - Discuss with your students why they will be using clickers. Describe how clickers typically improve student learning and enjoyment.
   - (Optional, but recommended) Stress that genuine learning is *not* easy and that clickers (and conceptual questions and conversations with peers) can help students find out what they don't really understand and what they need to think about further.
   - Quote some of the positive student comments from Chapter 9.
   - Discuss how you will assign clicker grades. Remember that students will start out focusing on the correct answer in each clicker use. If your emphasis is on discussion and learning the concept, tell them that *explicitly,* and describe what partial credit you intend to give for incorrect answers.
   - Explain what you will do when a student's clicker doesn't work, or if a student forgets to bring it to class. You can deal with that problem as well as personal problems that cause students to miss class by dropping the lowest clicker scores for each student.
   - Talk directly about cheating. Emphasize that using a clicker for someone else is like taking an exam for someone else and is cause for serious discipline. Explain what that discipline would be.

7. **Be prepared . . .**
   You are likely to have a considerably livelier and more interesting class than you have ever had before. Expect good results immediately but better results as you become more experienced with clickers.

8. **Be encouraged . . .**
Share your experiences, questions, and results with your colleagues and the author of this book.

One of the more thought-provoking pieces we've read concerning teaching science is the Millikan Award lecture of Edward (Joe) Redish of the University of Maryland (1998), "Building a Science of Teaching Physics." Redish asks, "Why does Science cumulate [advance] but the teaching of science not?" He argues that we usually fail to apply the scientific method to the teaching of science. When we think we have a good new hypothesis on how to teach, we need to have multiple people test it, critique it, and publish or share the results. Let's disseminate what we learn about using clickers, and help our teaching cumulate what works well.

Appendix 1

Sample Clicker Questions

(Correct answer given in boldface)

Please note that these are just samples; please check with your Addison-Wesley/Benjamin Cummings sales representative for information on sets of questions available for your course.

Demonstrations

A very powerful use of clickers is in association with classroom demonstrations. Science education research has shown that demonstrations are often much less effective than instructors hope in getting students to remember concepts. But their effectiveness can be greatly increased simply by getting students to *predict* the experiment outcome before the experiment is performed.

With the demonstrations, especially, it is very effective to have students discuss their predictions with each other before you ask the clicker questions. A sample prediction question is given below.

Subject: Physics or Astronomy

1. Suppose a beam of white light shines through a prism and makes a spectrum at the front of the class. If I take a red filter and put it in the beam, what will happen to the spectrum?
   a. All the colors turn red.
   b. All the colors except red disappear.
   c. All the colors except blue disappear.
   d. It depends on which side of the prism you put the filter—in the undispersed beam or in the dispersed beam.

Recall Questions

Recall questions test how well students have learned factual information, but they do not test whether the students understand the concepts which underlie the facts.

Subject: Astronomy

1. An *astronomical unit* is defined as
   a. 1,000 miles
   b. 1,000,000 miles
   c. The earth's distance from the sun
   d. The size of the solar system

2. When it is summer in the United States, in Australia it is
   a. Winter
   b. Summer
   c. It is always summer in Australia.

Conceptual Questions

Conceptual questions are designed to probe how well students actually understand a specific concept.

Subject: Astronomy

1. When astronauts are in the space shuttle, they can float around—they are "weightless." Why is that?
   a. There is no gravity in space.
   b. They are far enough from earth that gravity doesn't matter.
   c. **They are "falling" around the earth at the same rate as the shuttle, so they don't feel gravity's effects.**
   d. The gravity from other planets and the moon balances earth's gravity.

2. At the speed the astronauts traveled to the moon, how long would it take them to reach the nearest star, Alpha Centauri?
   a. About a month
   b. About a year
   c. About 10 years
   d. About 1,000 years
   e. **About 1,000,000 years**

(The boldfaced correct answer is designed to emphasize the concept that the spaces between the stars are enormously large, much larger than any distances in our solar system. Although numbers are mentioned, no calculation is required.)

3. If you made a scale model of the solar system using a grapefruit for the sun, the earth might be:
   a. An orange
   b. A grape
   c. **A grain of rice**
   d. A bacterium

4. If you made a scale model of the solar system using a grapefruit for the sun, the earth might be a grain of rice how far from the grapefruit:
   a. Two inches
   b. Four inches
   c. Four feet
   d. **Forty feet**

Subject: Chemistry

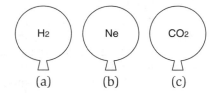

(a)   (b)   (c)

1. The balloons shown above each contain 1 liter of the specified gas at STP. What statement about the balloons is true:
   a. Balloon (a) contains the most moles of gas.
   b. Balloon (b) contains the most moles of gas.
   c. Balloon (c) contains the most moles of gas.
   d. All balloons contain the same number of moles of gas.

2. Which balloon weighs the most?
   a. Balloon (a)
   b. Balloon (b)
   c. Balloon (c)
   d. All three balloons weigh the same.

Subject: Environmental Science

1. Which statement is FALSE?
   a. The global population growth rate is decreasing.
   b. The global population is increasing.
   c. At a TFR of 2.4, a human population grows.
   d. Populations with age distributions skewed toward young people grow more slowly.

2. Do you think that all developed nations will necessarily complete the demographic transition and reach a permanent state of low birth and death rates?
   a. Definitely
   b. Probably
   c. Probably not
   d. Definitely not

3. Between which values of the percentage of school enrollment for females does TFR begin increasing?

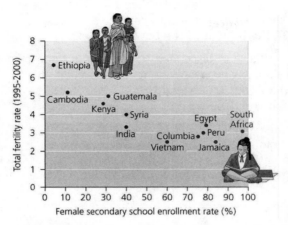

Source: Data from M. McDonald and D. Nierenberg, Linking population, women, and biodiversity, State of the World, Worldwatch Institute, 2003

    a. 10–30%
    b. 20–40%
    c. 40–60%
    d. 70–90%

4. Do you believe that national governments should implement policies, subsidies, or other programs to reduce birth rates?
    a. No, not at all
    b. Yes, but only positive incentives for fewer children
    c. Yes—penalties for too many children
    d. Yes, both incentives and penalties

(Questions 2 and 4 are designed for provoking discussion and have more than one correct answer.)

Subject: Physics

1. An object has zero velocity. Its acceleration
    a. Could be positive or negative.
    b. Must be zero.
    c. Could be positive, negative, or zero.

2. An object with density slightly higher than water is released into a bowl of water. It
   a. Floats with just a little of the object above the water.
   b. Floats slightly below the surface.
   c. Sinks to the bottom of the bowl.

3. An elevator that has descended from the 50th floor is coming to a halt at the 1st floor. As it does, your apparent weight is
   a. More than your true weight.
   b. Less than your true weight.
   c. Equal to your true weight.
   d. Zero.

4. A Martian lander is approaching the surface. It is slowing its descent by firing its rocket motor. Which is the correct free-body diagram for the lander?

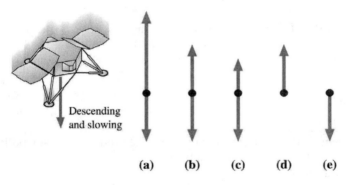

| (a) | (b) | (c) | (d) | (e) |

(a is correct)

Subject: Statistics and Data Analysis

Some student groups were given simple equipment and asked to make a measurement. Their results are shown in the figure. (Don't miss the data point showing that one group got 15.)

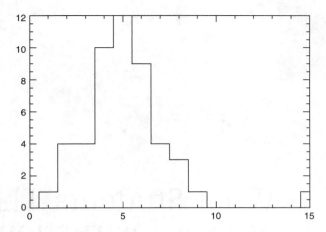

1. What is the *approximate* standard deviation of the measurements?
   a. About 2
   b. About 4
   c. About 5
   d. 9.5
   e. There is not enough information to estimate it.

2. Why didn't all the students get the same answer?
   a. Probably a lot of them made mistakes.
   b. All measurement involves random error; the distribution looks mostly like random errors.
   c. There is not enough information to tell.

3. What can you say about the group that measured the value 15?
   a. They were really unlucky; their result is many standard deviations from the mean.
   b. They must have made a mistake or a systematic error.
   c. We don't even know who made that measurement—how could we tell?

These data are from an actual student experiment. One group reported their answer in feet instead of meters!

Appendix 2

What Students Think of Peer Instruction

Chapter 6 provides information on what students think of clicker use. Much of that data comes from classes where clickers were used in conjunction with peer discussions between students. For those wondering about the importance of the peer interaction, the following results are reported. They are based on an 80-student introductory astronomy course for nonscience majors taught by the author for 4 years beginning in 1996. Clickers are often used in large introductory courses for nonmajors, so these results should have some general applicability. Since they were obtained before clickers were widely available, they show the results of peer instruction alone. Peer instruction had a substantial benefit, and we hope these results encourage readers to use clickers with peer discussions. Although the topic of this class was introductory astronomy, *the student attitudes about science are general.* Anyone teaching a large class of nonmajor students should think carefully about how peer instruction used with provocative, conceptual questions can improve students' attitudes as well as their learning.

A show of hands at the beginning of the course showed that only about 10–15% of the students said they liked science. We became curious to find out why so few students had a positive attitude about science, especially since one of the main course goals was for students to finish the class liking astronomy enough that they would continue to be interested in it throughout their lives. Course goals also included wanting them to genuinely understand the scientific process and to become able to apply scientific reasoning in their everyday lives. We therefore had a colleague in education interview students at the start of the course. The following comments came up repeatedly.

Reasons Students Say They Don't Like Science

1. I'm a creative person, so I'd like to do something creative. (Not science!)
2. I'm not good at math; I'm not good at science. (I can't do it.)
3. It is not at all relevant to my life. (Why should I do it?)
4. I like to do things that are involving, and that involve other people.

We were particularly surprised and disappointed by answer 1, since every scientist we know thinks science is creative! On reflection, however, we realized that the science students see in class is virtually all correct and highly sanitized. There is a "right" answer to almost every problem or lab. The exciting uncertainty when one isn't sure of the answer, the give and take that happens in scientific arguments and at meetings, and the "real" but messy parts of science are all hidden from them. What the comments show is that we are not giving students the real flavor of what we like about science, and that is a big part of why they don't like it.

We therefore began to look for ways to introduce more discovery, debate, and relevance into the curriculum. It is worth emphasizing that the changes made were small and designed to be done with relatively small investment of faculty time. We spent no more time with these classes than when we lectured the full class period. We just didn't talk the last 10–15 minutes of one class and about 10 minutes at the start of the next class. Our changes were twofold:

1) Each week we introduced a single "peer activity." Toward the end of the Tuesday lecture, the class was broken into groups and presented with a simple demonstration that was not completed. They were given about 10 minutes to discuss what would happen. At the beginning of the Thursday lecture, each student turned in a prediction of what they thought would happen. This was graded 1 or 0 (done, not done) or occasionally 2 (especially thoughtful) based on the reasoning expressed—not whether they got the correct answer. Since there were no clickers, the student responses were written out and collected. The demonstration was then performed. A number of demonstrations with surprising results were given, including ones that Aristotle got wrong (e.g., dropping a heavy object and a light object). Students clearly enjoyed the element of surprise.

2) On homework sets or in labs, we put a few problems that were specifically chosen to highlight everyday applications of science and math concepts taught in the class. For instance, a lesson on large numbers and scientific notation required calculations of an individual's fraction of the U.S. national debt rather than just masses of astronomical objects. Judging from student

remarks (they were shocked that their share of the national debt is over $20,000), this made a significant impression. In fact, more than a year following the class, students stopped us several times and brought up these problems and the demonstration predictions.

Our peer activities were similar to those of Mazur (1997), but fewer were used and the instructor preparation time consequently was less. Unlike his preengineering or premed students, ours did not have to cover a set curriculum, and we did not cover as much material as Mazur. In the beginning we wanted to start peer instruction a little at a time as we were novices. It is important to realize that you may start slowly as well.

At the end of the term all students were asked anonymously and in writing, "Did this class change your view of science in any way? If so, how?" In all 4 years, between 80 and 90% of students answered that their view of science had changed. A number of students suggested that they entered the class thinking scientists were almost always right. (After all, their instructors and textbooks were!) They could not meet this standard, so they thought they could not participate in scientific discussions. These comments caused us to realize that the parts of science we find the most motivating (questions where the answer is not yet known and passionate debate with colleagues over whose theory is right) are not what students experience in a standard class. The relatively small introduction of peer interaction, based on interesting and surprising demonstrations, addressed these failings of a standard class, and the effect on student attitudes was striking.

It seems clear that introductory courses could be enhanced, with modest effort, by:

1. Introducing open-ended activities that encourage creativity (e.g., experiments with surprising or open-ended results, projects, or writing).
2. Creating a "classroom climate" consistent with the goals. Students must know that it's OK to be wrong, to conjecture, to speculate—or most won't speak up.
3. Take advantage of peer pressure by using "peer instruction." That is by far the easiest way to get students much more involved in discussing and thinking about science.
4. Connect science principles to everyday life outside the classroom.

Four years of student responses to the question "Did this class change your view of science in any way? If so, how?" are summarized in the table below which is followed by representative student quotations.

Table A2.1

Year	1996	1997	1998	1999
Number of student responses	78	68	57	66

Question: Did this class change your view of science in any way? If so, how?

Student Response (given in percentage):

	1996	1997	1998	1999
My attitude about science did not change.	9	3	4	3
My attitude did change. . . .				
I found I could like science; it is interesting; it is not boring.	35	29	30	26
Science applies to my everyday life; it is relevant; it is useful outside of class.	18	18	25	15
I can do science; I can figure things out or reason scientifically, which I previously didn't believe.	18	16	18	17
I now understand the importance of data, experiment, prediction.	12	13	22	11
Science is creative, open-ended, not just memorization.	13	10	12	15
There is grandeur in the scientific study of the universe.	17	15	7	8
I now appreciate how much is unknown.	4	3	16	9
I want to study more astronomy.	4	6	5	5
I understand specific topics (in order of frequency mentioned): stellar evolution, cosmology, seasons or lunar phases, why the sky is blue, other.	24	9	12	18

Responses are percentages. They do not add up to 100 since some students gave more than one response.

Table A2.2 shows representative student answers to the question (asked at the end of the term), "Has this course changed your view of science in any way? If so, how?" We found it interesting that there appears to be no correlation between students' grades and comments about the course. Furthermore about 90% answered the question, "Yes it is interesting and open-ended, rather than boring. . . ."

Table A2.2
Student responses to the question: Has this course changed your view of science in any way? If so how?

Course grade	Answer
B	Yes, it has made science much more interesting mainly because of the debate and theory involved. I am intrigued by the fact that science does not have all the answers but can be used as the means to find them. I think it is very good when answers are found but they are still in question. This uncertainty keeps it going in the future.
C+	This class has actually made science fun again! Interesting topics, presented in a rigorous environment, have been a great success. As far as a view on science, it has definitely shown that the amazing thing about science is that everything is up for contest and that every conclusion reached, from recent ones to Einstein's special theory of relativity, can be falsified at any moment.
C−	Yes. I never saw science as being philosophical or theoretical . . . I mean all the other science classes I've taken have only required me to memorize stuff, whereas in this course I've had to think . . . hard.
B+	I've never "tried this at home" before, but in this class the three of us in Chamberlin were dropping cups of water, searching for prisms and otherwise gleefully driving the rest of the house nuts in the pursuit of science.
A	Yes it has. Science doesn't have to be boring number crunching and practice problems. In addition, scientists don't claim to be omniscient. Many are only as good as their last data.

A large number of student responses focused on their new found discoveries of how appropriate science can be and how applicable it is to their everyday lives. Table A2.3 and A2.4 show representative responses.

Table A2.3

Student Response: It is something *I* can do. . .

B	Science seems more approachable than it did earlier.
B	Yes, science can be fun and even understandable to the average "nonscience" person. In fact, I've learned that contrary to my nearly life-long belief, anyone can learn about something scientific, even a subject like astronomy. Science is helpful for everyone because it teaches us that, through hypothesis, experimentation, prediction and confirmation of predictions, we have an excellent way of not "fooling ourselves."
B	Yes, I not only have the confidence to talk about astronomy but more importantly I am now able to think scientifically, which enables me to challenge claims, analyze everyday data, and come to my own conclusions.
B +	This course has changed my view of science in many ways. I once looked at science as something to memorize and complain about. I now see science as something all around me. I find myself walking with my friends at night pointing to Jupiter and Saturn and telling them about the moons of Jupiter . . . In fact, I've learned more than I ever imagined in this class and I'm ready to tell everyone what I know.
B +	I learned I can actually understand some parts of science, which I once doubted my ability. I have also seen how science can be put to everyday life, or rather how much of our everyday life really is science. As I was studying for the final I came across a quote from Mark Twain's "Life on the Mississippi," which was in our book. I cannot remember it exactly but it had something to this effect: In science we look for one small fact yet end up with much more information. It was a wonderful quote that sums up science and my experience in this class.

Table A2.4

Student Response: It applies to my everyday life . . .

B +	Yes—this is the first time I've been able to recognize science in my everyday life. It has given me skills to figure out why things happen, which in turn, makes me much more aware.
A–	Yes it has made me more interested in questioning the things I read, see, and listen to. And given me the confidence in knowing that I can figure things out on my own.
C	Yes. It is not just useless data or memorization, it is something that I can apply to everyday life. It has renewed my interest in all sciences and also has given me info that my parents and relatives do not have. Thus allowing me to dazzle them with my intellect.
C	Yes, I've come to believe that science has a lot more to do with people on a daily basis than I used to think.
A–	Yes, it's funny to say but I think it will make me a better parent. Now I know how to answer "childlike" questions like why is the sky blue? or why the sun shines? with very "adultlike" answers.
A	It may sound silly, but I feel like science is do-able and interesting now. Before, all that science classes taught me were how to push around blocks on an inclined plane or how to draw some chemical compound, but not why I was drawing it. Application to my life is important to me. My roommate is constantly telling me how sexy of a subject calculus is but I think astrophysics is more so, because it's hands-on and there is still a lot to be found out.
A–	Yes, it definitely has. This has been the most interesting science class I've ever taken. I actually went on the Internet to learn more about space exploration, news and research. This class showed me that science can be cool. Also that I much prefer astronomers over physicists.

Appendix 3

Clicker Best Practices

Chapter 11 covers the practical aspects of using clickers in your classroom. Here are some points on the best strategies and uses of clickers recommended by Dr. Javed Iqbal, who has been instrumental in spreading the use of clickers at the University of British Columbia and other universities across Canada.

1. The main focus of the technology should be to enhance interactive teaching and not to use it as a tool to keep attendance or to give on-the-spot quizzes that count toward the final grade.
2. Keep the grade for in-class clicker quizzes low. A suggested number is 5% of the overall grade. A higher percentage leads to anxiety among students, and they will be more focused on getting the answer right rather than on thinking critically.
3. Avoid asking questions that require a calculation. Emphasis should be on the questions that enhance critical thinking, conceptual understanding, and active learning.
4. Keep the level of difficulty at an intermediate level—not so easy that the answer is trivial (e.g., What are the units for pressure in an MKS system?) or so difficult that the students have no clue and randomly select an answer.
5. Use the system on a regular basis—at least once a lecture or once a week. If the students know that you will be using the system as soon as class starts, they will be ready for it.
6. Make sure that peer discussion and cooperative learning are important components of your interactive teaching. Simply having students vote on a problem without peer-to-peer discussion is not effective.

7. The written part of examinations (midterms, finals etc.) should test students on their conceptual understanding of the subject matter. If the classroom focus is on the conceptual understanding and the students are examined only on their problem-solving skills, then the students would see no benefit to classroom discussion or the importance of thinking through a conceptual problem.

References

Bloom, B., ed., *Taxonomy of Educational Objectives: Book 1, Cognitive Domain*. New York: Longman, 1956.

Deeming, G., "Results from the Astronomy Diagnostic Test national project," *Astronomy Education Review*, 1(1), http://aer.noao.edu, (2001).

Duncan, D.K. home page: http://casa.colorado.edu/ ~ dduncan.

Duncan, D.K. 1999, "A challenging new way to teach astronomy: What to do in a large lecture class besides lecture?" *Mercury* (Astronomical Society of the Pacific), 28 (1). Available at http://casa.colorado.edu/ ~ dduncan.

Elby, A., "Helping physics students learn how to learn," *American Journal of Physics, Physics Education Research Supplement*, 69(7), S54–S64, (2001).

Hake, R.R., "Interactive engagement vs. traditional methods: A six thousand student survey of mechanics test data for introductory physics courses," *American Journal of Physics*, 66, 64–74, (1998).

Halloun, I.A., & Hestenes, D., "Common-sense concepts about motion," *American Journal of Physics*, 53, 1056–1065, (1985).

Hestenes, D., Wells, M., & Swackhammer, G., "Force Concept Inventory," *The Physics Teacher*, 30, 141–158, (1992).

Horowitz, H., *Interactivity in a classroom environment*, presented at the Sixth Conference of Interactive Instruction Delivery for the Society of Applied Learning Technology (SALT), (1988). Available on the Web site of eInstruction: http://www.einstruction.com/, under "News."

Mazur, E., *Peer instruction: A user's manual*, Pearson-Prentice Hall, (1997).

Mazur, E., 2004. Private communication.

McDermott, L.C. and E.F. Redish (1999), "Resource letter on Physics Education Research," *American Journal of Physics* 67 (9) 755.

Pollock, S., "Fighting the Fade: Student Engagement in Large Peer-Instruction Classes," available from the physics education research group, Univ. of Colorado, 2004. (www.colorado.edu/physics/EducationIssues).

Redish, E.F. 1999, "Millikan Lecture 1998: Building a Science of Teaching Physics," *American Journal of Physics* 67, 562.

Rogers, R., "Using personal response systems to engage students and enhance learning," in *Making statistics more effective in schools and business* conference, Georgetown University, http://www.umass.edu/cft/prs, (2003).

Schneps, M.H. and P.M. Sadler, "A Private Universe" and "Minds of Our Own," Harvard-Smithsonian Center for Astrophysics, Science Education Department, Science Media Group, 1987. Video available from Annenberg/CPB (www.learner.org).

Sokoloff, D.R., & Thornton, R.K., "Using interactive lecture demonstrations to create an active learning environment," *The Physics Teacher, 35*, 340–346, (1997).

Tobias, S., and Raphael, J., *The Hidden Curriculum*, Plenum Press, 1997.

Trees, A., & Jackson, M., "The learning environment in clicker classrooms: Student processes of learning and involvement in large courses using student response systems," Communications Department, Univ. of Colorado, (2003).

Weiman, C., & Perkins, K., unpublished study, Physics Department, University of Colorado (2004).